“Happy Couples Habits”

Brisk Banner

This book Happy Couples Habits, by Brisk Banner

Title: Happy Couples Habit

Author: Brisk Banner

Release Date: August, 2022

Language: English

This book is simply meant to spice up marriages, relationships, friendships etc.

Happy Couples Habits

Table of Contents:

HABITS OF HAPPY COUPLES

INTRODUCTION

Have you at any point thought about how blissful couples appear to have everything in perfect order? It's not generally simple to keep a cheerful relationship, but rather there are bunches of easily overlooked details you can do in your everyday lives that can help a ton. These propensities might appear to be basic on a superficial level, yet they've demonstrated to go quite far in your connections.

Having a decent relationship doesn't imply that you and your accomplice won't ever have clashes, or that every one of the issues in the relationship are settled or absolutely pleasing to you. Yet, when there's a persevering through association between you, your struggles with one another don't grow into fighting.

Nobody is great, and that incorporates your accomplice – however imagine a scenario in which there was a method for improving your relationship. Consider the possibility that these propensities were not only a logical truth from cheerful couples' exploration yet the way in to a more extravagant, really satisfying existence with the individual you love.

Bliss is the objective for so many of us, and these seven propensities can truly assist you with accomplishing it — so why not give them a shot? It could amaze you how much more joyful your life becomes.

HAVING TIME TOGETHER INTIMATELY

Supper is an incredible opportunity to interface and have profound discussions with your accomplice. You don't necessarily in every case need to discuss work and stress – you can likewise discuss arbitrary points you're into or that are fascinating to you. However long it's tomfoolery and not unpleasant, various points can truly assist with flavoring things up in your relationship.

Regardless of whether you're not the most ideal cook, making supper in some time is a higher priority than having the most ideal fixings that anyone could hope to find. Blissful couples live it up first and the food later. Imparting a dinner to somebody is a significant approach to interfacing on a cozy, non-sexual level. Talking and examining the unremarkable things that are vital to both of you is perfect for encouraging a bond.

Supper is likewise an incredible opportunity to show your accomplice the amount you esteem them. Other than the close to home advantage referenced above, eating with your accomplice every night can be a magnificent way to their significance. What's more, it doesn't need to be costly all things considered. Get imaginative with what you cook (heaps of individuals purchase an adequate number of canned or frozen food varieties to last the entire year and afterward serve them upstanding at dinnertime).

Drink a glass of wine consistently

Wine is great for the wellbeing and can assist with loosening up you following a distressing day, so it's a good idea to have some at night. The advantages of this one are really clear.

Be it grape, apple, or orange, drinking a glass of wine can prime you for sentiment. The synthetic compounds in liquor — explicitly the red assortment — can make an individual more loose and less unsure. This might help you open up and interface with your accomplice all the more without any problem. Blissful couples know a wine mysterious.

The liquor made them giggle and discuss dream situations. The mind's award framework becomes dynamic in reactions to fiction and sentiment.

All in all, whenever you're plunking down to supper with your darling, why not whip out the jug? You'll both rest easier thinking about it toward the beginning of the day. This could try and prompt somewhat more kissing.

Spend something like 30 minutes in a casual, connecting with movement together

Consider playing a couple's down or doing something connected with your side interests. Assuming you take part in an action that you ordinarily wouldn't do, you could get to know one another more. This can be an effective method for examining issues in your relationship since it's something you are both doing together, so the discussion might stream.

Nothing bad can really be said about hanging out and talking too. Assuming investing energy with your soul mate causes the person in question to feel cherished and appreciated, all that will go better for your relationship. Attempt to set aside a few minutes for these exercises as frequently as possible. On the off chance that you do this routinely, it will develop a solid groundwork for your relationship and keep on reinforcing it.

Assuming you've considered what the mystery is to being a couple like this, obviously, the response is that there isn't any one "secret." And truly any couple, regardless of how cheerful they show up, can run into serious difficulty. In any case, specialists truly do realize that there are sure propensities and approaches to conveying that appear to assist couples with feeling more fulfilled. In the event that you might want to build your own conjugal joy (and who doesn't?), have a go at making progress with up your propensities to incorporate a couple of these.

Sending Caring Messages

The vast majority of us text our accomplices essentially two or three times each day, and once in a while frequently. A large part of the time, these messages might be on the down to earth side — yet take a stab at setting aside a few minutes for a few simply cherishing, tender messages, as well. It just requires a second, and studies show it can improve your relationship.

Share The Stuff That Is important

It tends to be adequately hard to carve out opportunity to talk — and when we do, it could be about work, the children, family matter, or the house. However, there's serious areas of strength for a for venturing outside these natural subjects and into the domain of those greater, more significant points. You know... the ones you used to discuss back when you were dating. What's your fantasy get-away? How would you expect to be recalled? What side interest do you covertly need to begin? A huge investigation of couples found that the individuals who offer private subtleties like these are more joyful.

BE Actually Friendly Every DAY

In the buzzing about of day to day existence, we might neglect to dial back and actually associate with our mates. We're discussing sex here, yet a wide range of actual association, from handholding to long embraces to day to day kisses and strokes. Information show that individuals in genuinely friendly connections are more joyful and more fulfilled. (Incidentally, nestling and nonsexual friendship appear to mean quite a bit to men.)

TURN TOWARDS, NOT AWAY

Consistently, as we get to know one another, we offer little remarks and perceptions that "welcome" our mate to interface. Did you catch wind of that story in the news? This insane thing happened to me at work. Check this delightful dusk out! Specialists have found that individuals in cheerful connections answer these "offers" for association emphatically and transparently, while those whose connections are less blissful are bound to overlook or not answer. Consistently, make sure to turn towards, not away.

Observe AND HAVE Some good times TOGETHER

Hitched life can get going, insane, and now and then very task-arranged. Did you get the virus medication? And the laundry? We have parent-educator meetings this evening! However, assuming we neglect to set aside a few minutes for pleasure and tranquil great times together, we miss out.

Offer Thanks AND APPRECIATION On a more regular basis

When did you last thank your life partner for something the individual did? Sadly, at times we will quite often zero in on what our accomplices mess up, and neglect to say "much obliged" for all that they do well. In any case, appreciation and appreciation assume a key part in sustaining responsibility and holding connections together.

Work IN Additional Ceremonies

Adding a couple of several customs to your day, year, or routine can assist you two with building an exceptional common culture that is just about the couple. Whether it's "Wednesday Doughnut Day," a day to day dusk stroll with the canine, an evening time petition together, or the manner in which you commend the new ball season, these minutes will assist with making recollections and bring you closer.

Make sure TO Fix

Two or three battles and encounters issues, yet one variable that can truly have an effect, specialists find, is the means by which well we recuperate from these negative minutes. Next time things get somewhat "broken," make certain to bring a "fix" to the table with adoration, trustworthiness, and geniality. There can be 100 unique ways of doing this. The significant thing is to put forth the attempt with an open heart.

PRACTICE Irregular Thoughtful gestures

It might appear glaringly evident, yet in some cases we as a whole need an update: thoughtfulness counts. After some time, couples who exceed all expectations to help each other out in little ways (like topping off the vehicle with gas, doing the dishes in any event, when it's not "your turn," or getting those most loved biscuits at the pastry shop) are bound to be content than the people who aren't as liberal or kind with each other.

Hit the sack Simultaneously

Does one of you will generally trundle off to bed right on time while the other one stays up perusing, working, sitting in front of the television, or on the Web? It's a recognizable circumstance for bunches of couples- - particularly in the event that somebody needs to rise and shine early, or on the other hand in the event that one of you is a "evening person" while the other is a "songbird." Yet you should check whether you can improve on up this propensity, at any rate a portion of the time. Research recommends that couples who hit the sack simultaneously report less struggle, more serious discussion, and more sex. Time to cuddle up.

SET ASIDE A FEW MINUTES FOR ACTUAL FONDNESS

Couples who are most joyful might be the individuals who take time consistently to interface, especially genuinely. There are such countless advantages that actual closeness makes, like further holding and decreased pressure. Couples that make an everyday propensity for taking part in a critical embrace, who invest energy snuggling together, or participate in different kinds of actual closeness, including sex, report higher paces of bliss in their relationship.

It's to be expected, and you needn't bother with to be a clinician or researcher to comprehend the reason why actual closeness and fondness might really work out for us. Consider how ameliorating a hug feels. How sweet and basic clasping hands can be. Or then again the way that the time spent enveloped by one another's arms in bed can feel so mysterious.

Actual closeness doesn't generally come effectively to us. For certain couples, snuggling isn't in the everyday timetable, and that is not a problem. However, is it permitting them to be content in their relationship?

As people are physical, social individuals, it may be the case that you and your accomplice need to check all the more everyday actual closeness out. Until you hang out, you may not know the amount of a distinction it could make.

Actual Closeness Challenge: to coordinate more actual connection together into your relationship, take time this week to attempt to construct another propensity.

One choice is the 30-second kiss. For 30 seconds every day in the current week, you and your accomplice will meet for a long, waiting kiss.

Focusing on even a portion of a moment each day to zero in on your closeness and your relationship is significant. You truly can't do this activity without having a few advantages come from it. We're willing to wager you'll wind up partaking in this short experience without a doubt, and you may very well find it sets a completely unique tone for the afternoon.

Go strolling with your accomplice

This is a propensity that my better half and I have made where we have seen a more profound association in our relationship. On the off chance that you love nature and investing nature of energy with your accomplice, practice it regularly to go strolling — either in the mornings before you start your day, or in the nights. John and I stroll in the nights and Sunday mornings. It is a psychological choice that we make consistently to go strolling together. This advances discussion, quality time, and openness to natural air. When you lay out this propensity, your body will really need to go strolling. I've encountered this with John: Since we've regularly practiced it of strolling in the nights and Sunday mornings, my body longs for to invest that nature of energy. Strolling with your accomplice additionally advances great activity, and can be pretty much as straightforward as strolling up down your block and back. Choose with your accomplice how long and how frequently you might want to walk; the key variable is being in total agreement and ensuring that you settle on the psychological choice to lay out this propensity together.

DISCUSS EACH OTHER'S NEEDS

As a couple, how frequently do you expressly let your accomplice know it you're requiring or feeling? It very well might be on rare occasions than you naturally suspect.

So often, it's not difficult to feel like our accomplice ought to naturally "know'" what it is that we're thinking, feeling, or requiring. In any case, actually sentiments are chaotic and accomplices aren't mind readers. Indeed, even following 8 years with my better half, I actually can't necessarily in every case determine what it is that is happening in his mind. As natural as I trust myself to be, there's something else to find about him.

Be that as it may, what do cheerful couples do about this? They give it to one another straight.

At the point when I don't know what Nathan is feeling or requiring, I ask him straightforwardly. What's more, on the other hand, while I'm feeling focused on and could utilize some additional adoration, fondness, or time alone, I let him know similarly as straightforwardly.

Solid, blissful couples examine their necessities, needs, feelings, and everything with straightforwardness and sincerity. It's truly not confidential. The method for getting your necessities met and feel blissful, upheld, and secure, is to have the option to discuss those things without reservation. As far as I might be concerned, this is one of the main bits of relationship guidance for couples.

What's more, with regards to propensities, this is one that a couple ought to rehearse together every day. Make time every single day to examine what's the deal with you and how your accomplice could help. This kind of legitimate, open correspondence is extraordinary.

It might feel new right away, especially in the event that you're not accustomed to it. So begin little.

Sharing Your Necessities Challenge: opening up to your accomplice about stuff doesn't need to be muddled. For multi week, have a go at consolidating this as another relationship custom: take time each day or consistently (maybe just before you hit the sack) to share only one great and terrible thing that happened that day. Then share one thing about your accomplice that you're appreciative for.

Simply by presenting these 3 little snippets of data, you're making ready together to additional open exchanges. The subsequent stage? Asking each other how you could assist you cooperate with that awful thing that occurred. In any case, that is for the following week.

Switch off the TV in the nights and accompany your accomplice

How might you potentially associate with your accomplice when the TV is generally on? There is no association building when the both of you are continually gazing at the TV screen in the nights. Go with the psychological choice to switch off the television in the nights, and get to know one another. Sometimes, you can cuddle and watch a film, however try not to stare at the TV most nights. Carve out opportunity to get some information about their day and how they're doing. This propensity makes association and love. Cuddle up on the sofa and talk with your accomplice; discuss one another and how you two might foster your relationship. There will constantly be something to discuss, whether it's anticipating the following get-away or your next night out. Center around fostering your relationship, and discuss issues that should be tended to.

4. Acquire your accomplice espresso the morning

This straightforward motion is a seriously big deal to my better half. He appreciates drinking espresso, and acquiring it to him the morning communicates love and fondness. Assuming your accomplice likes to savor espresso the morning, make this propensity and express love through this demonstration of administration. While I present to John some espresso, it shows that I give it a second thought, and that this is one way I can cherish him. Awaken a couple of moments prior so you and your accomplice can get to know each other prior to going to work. This is a straightforward yet strong propensity for cheerful connections.

Express certain qualities about your accomplice to other people

The propensity for communicating positive ascribes about your accomplice will assist with extending the association in your relationship. Going against the norm, communicating negative credits about your accomplice will just form a tall wall among you. Do you know a couple that generally contends in broad daylight and communicates negative characteristics about one another to companions? This is a persistent vice that in the long run obliterates a relationship. This negative example of conduct makes doubt, separation and absence of regard. Make a propensity for communicating positive credits to other people. This positive example of conduct makes reverence, affection and love.

Reconnect over the course of the day

We have such bustling timetables that interfacing with your accomplice over the course of the day can be last need, yet if you need to have a cheerful, durable relationship, reconnecting with your accomplice over the course of the day is essential. It tends to be essentially as straightforward as sending a caring message during your mid-day break or calling your accomplice coming back. This propensity is intended to keep the association and concentration with your accomplice. Regardless of whether you have a rushed timetable, you can in any case make an opportunity to spend an instant message or give your accomplice a call. Be innovative. Consider ways that you can do to reconnect with your accomplice over the course of the day.

Praise each other day to day

Seeing the easily overlooked details is simple. New and not new connections can profit from day to day praises. This can assist with helping you to remember how fortunate you're to have your accomplice. Blissful couples generally praise each other for words and activities.

Offer commendations in view of your accomplice's own character rather than conventional or shallow ones that don't exactly make a difference. Remember to see the value in yourself, as well. Fearlessness is a significant piece of joy.

Praise your accomplice's achievements. We frequently base our connections on unadulterated inclination like love or physical allure. Now and again it's ideal to realize that you're valued for your endeavors.

"I'm so pleased with you for getting an advancement at work."

"Much obliged to you for welcoming me to your family party; I lived it up."

"You generally track down incredible modest flights."

It's memorable essential that similarly as we value difficult work and victories, others appreciate when we do likewise for them.

The more genuine and explicit you can be, the better your commendation will be. Working out a couple is an incredible method for arranging what you need to say. Utilize these notes all through the year with your accomplice or save them close by for a fitting second.

Continuously recognize your accomplice

Recognizing your accomplice is a propensity that merits making, as it's a fundamental element for making a cheerful, solid and enduring association. At the point when you express regard towards your accomplice, you are communicating your affection, acknowledgment, and warmth. At the point when you express disregard, you are communicating that you don't acknowledge your accomplice. Regarding your accomplice is tied in with esteeming them for who they are, including contrasts. You might have an alternate point of view yet this doesn't imply that you ought to slight your accomplice and put them down.

At the point when you experience conflicts, ensure that you regard your accomplice's disparities. This doesn't permit you to disregard your accomplice out in the open or before loved ones. Continuously extend regard particularly when you have a conflict. There will be times where you disagree on an issue and it will be the means by which you handle this issue as a group that will have a significant effect.

Triumph ultimately the final says regarding a contention (to some degree once in a while)

Settling contentions soundly is vital for blissful couples. One method for doing this is by tackling issues and tending to worries collectively — but at the same time it's acceptable for you to triumph ultimately the final say regarding a contention sometimes. Simply make an effort not to mean it that way. Know where the line is between protecting your situation and being cautious.

Triumph ultimately the final says regarding a contention to work on your connections and win your life partner's adoration and friendship.

A straightforward contention about who neglected to stack the dishwasher isn't a crisis, so taking a break is superfluous.

Blissful couples need to triumph ultimately the final say regarding a contention since it can assist with settling issues before they develop any more hatred than they as of now have. You triumph ultimately the final word when you settle a contention by winning your accomplice back.

In some cases, individuals are obstinate to the point that they'll offer something terrible to get a response from their accomplices. In any case, some of the time, they're simply attempting to get a reaction, and afterward they pivot and utilize that against them later. This isn't relationship-building. In the event that you can't allow the individual to triumph when it's all said and done the final word, basically allow them an opportunity to talk.

Indeed, even the best romantic tales have stories of trouble, torment, and disunity. Battling is a typical piece of any marriage or relationship. Furthermore, genuine love frequently requests it. Yet, blissful couples have figured out how best to manage that contention when it emerges. This is a tremendous piece of keeping a fruitful relationship. For such couples, struggle doesn't mean something bad, however simply presents a potential chance to learn and become together.

Cheerful couples generally recall that they are in the same boat. At the point when a contention emerges, they know that it's both of them together against the issue, not both of them against each other. This idea alone can have a major effect in the result of a conflict (or even forestall one out and out).

So what do these couples realize about battling that you don't?

It very well may be a ton of things. Dealing with struggle well, first of all, isn't something that works out coincidentally. The best couples realize that a relationship takes work, and refereeing can be a significant piece of this. All in all, the couple that knows how to battle fair has likely invested the effort. They've contended over and over and found devices and approaches that work for themselves and for their relationship.

For your purposes, this implies that compromise abilities require some investment. What's more, that is totally fine. Everything thing you can manage is continue to dive deeper into solid clash and apply the standards you learn.

Likewise, center around those fundamental things, abilities that the vast majority of us know can assist with struggle: Don't hold feelings of resentment. Try not to raise old issues during your ongoing battle. Cool your heads prior to examining an issue together. Know about your words.

With each battle, assuming you try to turn out to be better at settling relationship struggle, you'll find that the enhancements stack up. All things considered, this is the way propensities are shaped!

Battle Fair Test: Make an objective for yourself this week that you'll adopt an alternate strategy in a contention circumstance. Be a sharp onlooker and find out how this turns out.

Communicate in your accomplice's way to express affection each and every day

Gary Chapman composed an extraordinary book on the5 main avenues for affection in which couples can communicate and encounter their language of affection and fondness. While taking a gander at these 5 ways to express affection, get some margin to figure out how you feel most cherished and how your accomplice feels most love. Envision you have an affection tank within you. Each time your accomplice talks your way to express affection, your adoration tank is being filled. Each time your accomplice doesn't communicate your main avenue for affection, your adoration tank runs short. With regards to strong propensities for blissful connections, making the propensity for talking your accomplice's way to express affection consistently lays out adoration, friendship and warmth in your relationship.

Cooking and cleaning

It's in every case significantly more fun when you cook with your accomplice. I realize that I appreciate cooking significantly more when John assists. The propensity for cooking together makes closeness, association and love; making and eating food turns into a cozy demonstration when you are with your accomplice. I express my affection through cooking and eating with my significant other (with the TV off), which fabricates a more profound association between us. This is an ideal chance to hang out.

In the event that you or your accomplice lean towards doing the cooking, make it a propensity that the other individual cleans. A propensity that John and I do is that at whatever point I cook, he tidies up subsequently, as well as the other way around. At the point when John tidies up after I cook, it shows appreciation for my cooking and that he esteems me. You actually should constantly appreciate and esteem your accomplice, regardless of whether it's pretty much as straightforward as cleaning the dishes. It's good to realize that John values the adoration that I put in my cooking and needing to do the dishes is an indication of affection warmth.

Express appreciation to your accomplice consistently

Value your accomplice! That's all there is to it. Anyway you need to communicate appreciation in your relationship, make it happen. Do it each and every day. With regards to strong propensities for cheerful connections, it's tied in with communicating your appreciation to your accomplice. This can be leaving an affection note prior to going to work or bringing back blossoms toward the finish of the affection. This returns to communicating in your accomplice's main avenue for affection. Figure out your accomplice's main avenue for affection and express your appreciation for your accomplice through their way to express affection. Assuming your accomplice feels move adored by nature of time, ensure that when you return home from work, "Mood killer" and concentrate on your accomplice. Sit on the lounge chair and simply accompany your accomplice. Whichever main avenue for affection that your accomplice talks, ensure that you communicate in a similar language. Practice it regularly of showing appreciation to your accomplice each and every day.

Cooperate collectively towards objectives (short and long haul)

A cheerful relationship centers around short and long haul objectives. These objectives are both for every person and furthermore as a team. Despondent couples don't have anything to anticipate throughout everyday life. They simply throw away their life on shallow hogwash and attempting to satisfy society's norm of bliss. Center inside your relationship around making, laying out and achieving objectives. Cheerful couples have objectives that are both little and enormous.

Invest nature of energy in the first part of the day to reflect and accompany accomplice prior to beginning the day

It's not difficult to get into a preparation routine wherein you awaken, have breakfast, go to work, return home, have supper, sit in front of the television, nod off and start from the very beginning again the following day. This routine most certainly begins depleting your relationship and the association that you have with your accomplice. We have such bustling timetables that it's significantly more critical to require investment in the mornings and reflect with your accomplice. Center around what united both of you and value that. It's not difficult to permit pressure, disappointment and interruptions to hinder having a blissful relationship, yet when you take the time in the mornings to cherish and value your accomplice, you are laying out a propensity that is loaded up with warmth, friendship and care.

Cuddle in the mornings and nights

Get some margin to cuddle prior to beginning your day and prior to heading to sleep. This can be pretty much as basic as holding each other in bed for a couple of moments prior to beginning the day. Did you had any idea that actual touch delivers a chemical called Oxytocin? The more you experience actual touch with your accomplice, your oxytocin level increments. Following a lot of time work, take time prior to heading to sleep and nestle.

Be available to unconstrained dates

Unconstrained dates are extraordinary in light of the fact that they allow you an opportunity to escape the house and accomplish something fun with your accomplice that doesn't actually need a lot of thought. This is perfect for pressure alleviation and significant on the off chance that you just moved in together.

There are numerous dates types you should seriously think about for your unconstrained thought.

Calm dates

This sort of date is perfect to zero in on your relationship, examine your sentiments and possess some energy for yourself. Calm dates are ideal on the off chance that you're feeling down or have to escape the house since something unpleasant occurred. For instance: in the event that one individual was rammed with work or school-related issues, that individual could go on a tranquil date without stressing over their accomplice's sentiments or timetables disrupting everything.

The most effective way to tell how well your calm date went is by taking a gander at the mirror and perceiving how blissful you appear when you return home. That ought to be a decent pointer.

Fun dates

Fun dates are perfect on the off chance that you've been separated for some time, need a break from one another. Fun dates are brilliant assuming you're worn out on doing likewise old things with your accomplice and you need some assortment. These dates are huge for exploring new territory that you've never finished or attempting to accomplish something together that you've fizzled at before.

An illustration of this sort of date would be hitting up a show together — or on the other hand on the off chance that you could do without shows, attempt an alternate sort of presentation, similar to the drama. One more thought for a tomfoolery date is to restrict your discussion with one another and perceive how much tomfoolery and happiness you can escape being in one another's presence.

In the event that you weren't one of the blissful couples previously, fun dates can bring new sentiments into your everyday practice.

Acknowledge Each Other's Shortcomings (Regardless of Whether It's Hard)

Indeed, even in cheerful couples, partners commit errors. In some cases, an accomplice could goof and commit an error that you don't appreciate. Perhaps you have done likewise that has made them anxious. Nothing bad can really be said about tolerating each other for what our identity is, regardless of whether it is noticeably flawed all of the time. Nobody is awesome, professing to the point that they can cause gives later on when they drive you up the wall.

While it very well might be difficult to concede when somebody you love has accomplished something you track down unsatisfactory or destructive, it's absolutely worth the work. Tolerating each other for what our identity is will assist you with seeing each other better and reinforce your relationship.

Thrashing yourself for your missteps won't help you not too far off. It's vital to invest the majority of your energy contemplating how to improve from now on.

People are flawed. We will commit errors, goof, and hurt others — regardless of how diligently we attempt to keep away from it. We are in general attempting to overcome this insane life. There is no disgrace in committing an error from time to time. It's totally standard, truth be told.

ACTIVITIES FOR HAPPY COUPLES

Love: the delightful way to track down it, how to keep it, and how to be content in it, is perhaps of the most examined and contemplated subject in our reality.

What makes for a cheerful relationship? How would I make a blissful relationship? The response to these inquiries is complicated. Sentiments regarding the matter could-and do-fill great many books.

While there might be nobody amazing response, throughout the long term designs have arisen. In sound and blissful connections, couples frequently show comparative characteristics or ways of behaving, across ages and even societies. We see consistently that there are exceptionally unequivocal propensities that a few couples take on which appear to bring about a fantastic, enduring relationship

They Focus On Their Relationship — Month to Month, Week After Week, And Day to Day

It's a relationship legend that marriage doesn't take work. It takes a ton of it! However, it's the most beneficial work there is.

Indeed, even with your perfect partner or the "great" accomplice, you'll rapidly find that a drawn out relationship requests work and exertion. This is definitely not something terrible. Rather, it's something astounding. Connections transform us and make us into better individuals. That is a marvelous result. Furthermore, simultaneously, they assist us with building cheerful lives loaded up with adoration.

This work doesn't need to be a trudge, in any case. A large part of the time (and preferably, more often than not) connections are simple, light, and happy. Work is as yet occurring, yet it's a greater amount of the in the background support work that is going on.

Indeed, one of the propensities for joyfully wedded couples is precisely this: a pledge to stay aware of that relationship work consistently. As such, focusing on the organization consistently.

This propensity is less about activity than about mentality. While activities are most certainly a pivotal piece of building these two or three propensities, this one requests the right mentality. It's tied in with simply deciding (huge and little) that emphasis on the prosperity of the relationship. It's the point at which you ensure that you're making opportunity to be together and mindful. It's the point at which you decline a solicitation to a night out with companions since you realize that night out hasn't occurred in some time, and you perceive that hanging out is so significant. That multitude of little activities, springing from the right outlook, accumulate into areas of strength for a, and a reasonable feeling of needs.

Need Challenge: Timetable a "marriage meeting" for quite a while in the following week. Here, you and your accomplice will really look at in about your relationship. If conceivable, concoct a few thoughts on how you can each work on in specific viewpoints. Examine your next unique night out together.

They Appreciate Each Other

Blissful couples routinely show each other their appreciation.

Nathan and I share our day to day thanks consistently before we head to sleep, and it's an extraordinary method for feeling associated and appreciated.

However, you don't need to show your appreciative hearts precisely like that. There are such countless ways of showing your gratefulness to your accomplice, and to ensure they realize they have your affection and your appreciation.

Kind words and praises are dependably welcome, obviously, however your accomplice might best get love and appreciation in alternate ways. This is where knowing your accomplice's main avenue for affection can prove to be useful. In the event that your accomplice communicates in the language of actual touch, for example, a delicate embrace after he's finished something supportive around the house can express stronger than words.

Or on the other hand, perhaps she will feel your adoration most profoundly when you make her a high quality gift. These basic articulations of appreciation are significant, yet what makes the biggest difference of all, is that you share them. Anyway you make it happen, try consistently to tell your accomplice how wonderful they are, and the amount you treasure them.

Appreciation Challenge: Challenge yourself each day to ponder one way you could show your accomplice you love and value them today. Then do it.

THEY Assume the best

Maintain that a straightforward way should stir something up? Be dubious.

Such countless contentions start this exact same way: an accomplice accomplishes something which adversely affects you, puts you in a bad mood, and so on. Some unacceptable reaction is to rush to make judgment calls, expecting your accomplice has awful aims and made a such move intentionally, maybe in any event, significance to hurt you. Is this consistent? Is this sensible? Likely not, except if you're living in a poisonous relationship.

In by far most of connections, accomplices need simply awesome for one another. Obviously, we people are chaotic, ridden with shortcomings, and very responsible to screw up. Be that as it may, in our souls, we decide and make moves in light of adoration and sincere goals.

What do blissful couples do? they recollect this! At the point when awful things occur, solid couples decide in favor trust. They assume the best about their accomplice. They don't focus in on fault. They don't index previous oversights and blames and afterward show them once more when their accomplice makes a blunder. All things being equal, they center around the affection that ties them together, and recall that the method for building something more grounded is to continuously move towards that adoration and towards trust.

Opportunity to be vindicated Test: Practice absolution this week. There might be a day or an occurrence in which your life partner says or accomplishes something frightful. (Furthermore, can we just be real, they most likely will, and you presumably will, as well). Yet, focus on elegance and deciding in favor trust. You may be stunned how much lighter you feel when you come at things according to this alternate point of view.

THEY DON'T Disregard Taking care of oneself

Shockingly, one of the main sound marriage propensities includes the people and not the couple. That is the propensity for taking care of oneself.

You can't carry your best to the relationship in the event that you're not dealing with yourself. What's more, the equivalent goes for your accomplice. The people who practice ordinary taking care of oneself can offer their absolute best that would be useful.

Marriage includes addressing the necessities of your accomplice yet it doesn't mean dismissing your own. In connections, we should continuously be trying to watch out for our physical, close to home, and mental necessities.

What's the significance here? This can mean numerous things! It might imply that you must save alone opportunity in your day or week, permitting you to re-energize and reboot. Or then again, it could mean you want to plan customary evenings with companions to have some friendly time.

It could imply that you want to investigate seeking treatment. Assuming you're battling for certain things (and who isn't) important for taking care of oneself might include tracking down a magnificent advisor to assist you with arranging of these issues. It could mean ensuring you hit the hay at a sensible hour, hydrate, and take your multivitamin.

Taking care of oneself can likewise mean simply setting aside a few minutes for yourself: for the things you love and the exercises you appreciate. Does the cheerful couple generally share normal interests? Not generally. This is absolutely OK. Yet, don't disregard the things you love regardless of whether your accomplice isn't that enthused about them. It is really beneficial to have separate interests, as a matter of fact. You totally don't have to do everything together to have a magnificent marriage and an extraordinary romantic tale.

STRONG PROPENSITIES FOR BLISSFUL CONNECTIONS

Propensities can have a strong effect in your relationship. The meaning of a propensity is: "a predictable and normal example of conduct". You can either make positive propensities or negative propensities, and when you begin rehearsing them, they will ultimately turn into a demonstration that is oblivious. With regards to having a cheerful relationship, there are sure propensities that can have a strong and positive effect. You genuinely should be compactness while making schedules, particularly for your relationship. You should really try each and every day to rehearse them so they become natural to you. It requires around 21 days to lay out a propensity, whether it's sure or negative. In this article, I will impart to you 12 strong propensities for blissful connections. These propensities have helped both in my marriage, and for the couples that I have worked with. Carry out every one of these propensities in your relationship and begin reconnecting with your accomplice.

A cheerful couple is definitely not a 'ideal couple' that meets up, yet a blemished couple that figures out how to partake in one another's disparities, and cooperates consistently to make something uniquely great. At the end of the day, an extraordinary relationship isn't karma and doesn't simply occur - it requires exertion and mind to persevere and develop in manners that keep the two accomplices satisfied.

Throughout the last 10 years, among us, Marc and I have perused many books on connections, trained a huge number of couples who were battling to track down satisfaction in their connections, and cooperated with more than 100,000 supporters (buy in here) who keep on asking us inquiries and enlighten us stories consistently concerning their connections.

All of this has given us sharp understanding into the particular ways of behaving that satisfy two individuals as a team. We've in a real sense watched couples go from "prepared to separate" to being "joyous beyond words" surprisingly fast, basically by making unpretentious, viable changes to their day to day propensities.

Of course however, when these couples get it sorted out, their newly discovered relationship propensities become natural to them, and accordingly, they never discuss them. Spectators might observer their public presentations of fondness and satisfaction, however stay dumbfounded with respect to the wellspring of their bliss. So that is exactly the very thing I need to examine today - the propensities cheerful couples have, however never discuss.

1. They practice taking care of oneself as people. - Connections don't make satisfaction, they reflect it. Satisfaction comes from the inside. Connections are just reflections of the consolidated delight that two individuals have as people. What you find in the mirror is what you find in your connections. Your failure in your accomplice frequently mirror your mistake in yourself. Your acknowledgment of your accomplice frequently mirrors your acknowledgment of yourself. Consequently, the initial step to having a solid relationship with another person is to have a sound connection with yourself.

2. They stand together and decline to allow outcasts to give orders. - Connections don't necessarily in every case check out, particularly from an external perspective. So don't allow outcasts to run your relationship for you. Assuming you're disapproving of your accomplice, sort out it with THEM and no other person. You need to carry on with your own lives your own specific manner... it's just as simple as that. Every one of us has an extraordinary fire in our heart for that one exceptional individual. It's our obligation, and our own alone, to choose if a relationship is.

1. They regard their relationship just like a novel, unique bond. - Don't contrast your relationship with any other individual's - not your parent's, companion's, associate's, or that arbitrary couple whose relationship appears to be awesome. Several makes their own affection rules, love arrangements, and love propensities. Simply center around what both of you offer, and create your extraordinary bond all that it tends to be. What's more, remember that all connections have their promising and less promising times - they don't ride at a ceaseless happy high. Cooperating through the tough situations will make your relationship more grounded eventually.

2. They are cozy about everything. - Sex isn't love. Particularly in the start of a relationship, fascination and joy in sex are frequently confused with adoration. Sex is great, sex is perfect, yet it's the simple aspect. Makes connections last closeness. It requires fair correspondence and receptiveness about worries, fears and misery, as well as expectations, dreams and bliss.

3. They acknowledge one another, without attempting to change one another. - The most profound hankering of human instinct is the

should be valued with no guarantees. Some of the time we attempt to be stone workers, continually cutting out of our life partners the picture of what we maintain that they should be - what we assume we really want, love, or want. Yet, these activities and discernments are against the real world, against their advantage and our own, and consistently end in frustration, since it doesn't fit them. The groundwork of adoration is to allow those we to think often about be proudly themselves, and to not contort them to accommodate our own pretentious thoughts of who they ought to be. In any case we fall head over heels just with our own dreams, and consequently pass up a great opportunity totally on their actual magnificence. So save your relationship from unnecessary pressure. Rather than attempting to change your accomplice, give them your help and become together.

4. They make continuous time for one another. - Assuming that you disregard your relationship, your relationship will disregard you as well. With occupied plans we frequently neglect to unwind and partake in the extraordinary organization we have. In connections distance isn't estimated in that frame of mind, in warmth. Two individuals

can be right close to one another but then miles separated. So don't overlook the one you love, since absence of concern frequently harms more than irate words.

5. They get out whatever they endlessly intend what they tell one another. - Your accomplice isn't telepathic. Share your contemplations. Give them the data they need as opposed to anticipating that they should know the mysterious. The more that stays implicit, the more prominent the gamble for issues. Begin conveying plainly. Try not to attempt to guess what they might be thinking, and don't make them attempt to peruse yours. Most issues, of all shapes and sizes, inside a relationship, begin with terrible correspondence.

6. They listen eagerly prior to answering. - Don't tune in so you can answer, pay attention to comprehend. Open your ears and psyche to your accomplice's interests and feelings without judgment. View at things according to your accomplice's point of view as well as your own.

7. They don't mess around with one another's heads and hearts. - Cheating and lying aren't battles, they're reasons couples separate. Since incredible things self-destruct

effectively when they've been kept intact with lies. In all actuality, connections don't do any harm; lying, cheating and curving reality until it plays with somebody's feelings harms. Guarantees mean the world, yet after they're broken, sorry makes very little difference (to some extent at first). So never screw with your accomplice's sentiments since you're uncertain of your own. Assuming you are uncertain in any capacity, make certain to say as much. Continuously be transparent. What's more, recall that when the fact of the matter is supplanted by quietness, quietness turns into a falsehood as well

8. They practice the brilliant rule in their relationship. - In a solid relationship, you get what you put in. You get nothing less and that's it. There is no space for self-centeredness. Assuming you need love, give love. If you have any desire to see a grin, give a grin. Try not to be worried about who's correct; be worried about cherishing and being adored, mindful and being really focused on.

9. They cheer for one another. - Having an appreciation for how astonishing your accomplice is prompts great spots - useful, satisfying, serene spots. So be glad for them

while they're gaining ground. Applaud their triumphs. Commend their achievements, and empower their objectives and aspirations. Challenge them to be all that they can be. Furthermore, be grateful for their favors, transparently.

10. They survey and examine their objectives and dreams frequently. - For couples, it's two against the world. Having ordinary conversations with one another about objectives, dreams, interests and the future, such that is positive and rousing, won't just unite you, however will likewise carry your aggregate cravings nearer to the real world.

11. They arrange and think twice about joint matters. - Since individuals' necessities are liquid and change after some time, and life itself requests change as well, the internal functions of good connections are arranged and yet again haggled constantly. Furthermore, periodically a two-way compromise is the best arrangement.

12. They decline to refuse to accept responsibility for the issues at hand. - Accusing doesn't achieve anything. Assume a sense of ownership with your activities. Assume a sense of ownership with your

relationship - the great times and the terrible. Work with your accomplice. Impart. Accusing them is a copout that doesn't achieve anything. Possibly you both take equivalent responsibility for issues both of you experience, or the issues will claim both of you.

13. They don't make a huge deal about things. - Individuals commit errors. Poo occurs. There's not a great explanation to break your relationship into pieces over spilt milk. One method for checking in the event that something merits considering is to pose yourself this inquiry: "Will this matter in one year's time?" In the event that not, then, at that point, let it go right away.

14. They manageable their indignation the moment they feel warmed. - Warmed contentions are a waste. Your accomplice doesn't need to be off-base for you to be correct. There are numerous streets to common decency. What's more, more often than not it simply doesn't make any difference that much. At the point when you feel outrage flooding up and you need to holler that foul comment barely out of reach of your mind, simply close your mouth and leave. Try not to allow your displeasure to outwit you. Give

yourself a chance to quiet down and afterward delicately examine what is going on.

15. They apologize to one another right away. - Posing up after a viewpoint is fundamental to each blissful relationship. A straightforward, genuine "Please accept my apologies" is generally the main step. We as whole commit errors, yet our readiness to just let it out doesn't generally fall into place. So recall, it doesn't exactly make any difference who's thinking correctly - what's right matters. Assuming your relationship is essential to you, a statement of regret is in every case right.

16. They practice persistence and absolution every day. - Statements of regret should be upheld by true tolerance and absolution. Since regardless of how fair and kind you attempt to be, you will at times offend your accomplice. What's more, this is definitively why persistence and absolution are so imperative to connections. Persistence is essentially the capacity to let your light gleam on the one you love, even after your wire has blown. Furthermore, pardoning is realizing where it counts that they didn't intend to blow your wire in any case.

17. They make everyday penances for one another. - Personal bonds are attached with

genuine affection, and genuine romance includes consideration, mindfulness, discipline, exertion, and having the option to think often about somebody and penance for them, ceaselessly, in endless frivolous minimal unsexy ways, consistently. You put your arms around them and love them in any case, in any event, when they're not entirely adorable. Furthermore, obviously they do likewise for you. To understand what a sound relationship is, it's one where two individuals get up each day and say, "This is worth the effort. All of you are worth the effort. I'm cheerful you are a major part of my life." It's about penance. It's tied in with realizing that a few days you should do things you abhorrence to make the one you love grin, and feeling impeccably pleased to do as such.

18. They regard each other's humanness. - Even the most joyful couples on Earth are still only two people. And all people are defective. On occasion, the sure lose certainty, the patient lose their understanding, the liberal demonstration self-centered, and the proficient second think about what they know. It could happen to potentially anyone. We commit errors, we blow our top, and we get found out unsuspecting. We stagger, we slip,

and we go crazy at times. In any case, that is the most exceedingly awful of it; we as a whole have our minutes. More often than not we're momentous. So stand adjacent to the one you love through their difficult seasons of flaw. In the event that you're not able to, you truly don't merit being around for their ideal minutes all things considered.

IDEAS IN RETROSPECT

By ordering this rundown I'm not recommending that these are the main keys to being a blissful couple, I'm just revealing insight into a few normal propensities that can have a significant effect. A lot of bliss in our connections is because of deliberate movement. Hence, it's workable as far as we're concerned to fundamentally further develop our adoration life basically by modifying what we decide to do consistently. Furthermore, a lot of what we do, both as couples and as people, we do on autopilot in light of our propensities.

Primary concern: Cheerful couples love one another. Furthermore, cherishing somebody isn't just about saying it consistently - it's tied in with showing it consistently all around.

Below are some of the experiences shared by cheerful couples;

Following 8 years, we are as yet learning and building in view of a large number of these characteristics. It requires investment, work and exertion and every one of these propensities fabricates and changes as we develop. Various forfeits or method for correspondence foster in various stages throughout everyday life. It is satisfying to be purposeful about keeping a sound relationship. Much thanks to You!

Number 4 is an incredible update for me. As a person, I generally need to deal with my eagerness to be more close with my sentiments and open about my viewpoints!

In light of your inquiry, one propensity that has helped my marriage is the taking care of oneself standard you plate in number 1. At the point when you get some down time to adore yourself, you can share that affection and satisfaction together. The self-esteem segment of your book has helped me and my significant other out colossally around here. We've really featured a few statements and we both use them as taking care of oneself certifications.

Actually, it begins with us. So frequently, we need to fix the other individual, yet we don't set aside some margin to adore ourselves or fix how we respond to who we accept our accomplice ought to be.

Gratitude for another incredible post

A portion of the little pieces of relationship guidance in this post hit home amazingly.

Much thanks to you for keeping me thinking, and keeping my psyche straight.

Subsequent to being hitched for 27 years this year, I can genuinely say that the fair correspondence you notice in your fourth and seventh focuses is the critical in my marriage. Assuming two individuals are in total agreement, they can overcome nearly anything together. You don't need to continuously concur; however you really do need to know where each other stand.

We regard each other's disparities. We see each other through the eyes of a kid, we actually date, we have breaks and breathers. We supplicate together. Also, we chuckle at each other and one another. We experience every day carefully and don't fixate a lot of tomorrow.

What a brilliant gathering.

You completely nailed it with all of the propensities.

There's something different that assisted me foster an excellent relationship with my better half.

Never condemn my significant other. Put her in every case first.

At first it could appear to be unthinkable. Or on the other hand even a too large penance of yourself.

In any case, let me make sense of.

You are very much aware of the result of censuring your mate. What's more, when she believes she's not at the highest point of your needs. There's no getting away from it.

She becomes melancholy. She grimaces at you. What's more, some of the time you even don't have the foggiest idea why.

So that is precisely exact thing happened to me.

However, when I began putting her first. What's more, when I quit condemning her. Our connections soar to an altogether new level.

Presently my better half has a steady grin all over. She chuckles routinely.

What's more, in this present circumstance it's simple for me to see when I screw up. At the point when I become narcissistic. At the point when I begin reprimanding her.

However, when I don't mess up, I don't need to request that my better half possess alone energy for my imaginative undertakings. She PUSHES me to have that. She's content with me seeking after my own fantasy and energy.

These 2 propensities notwithstanding those you referenced have assisted me keep a brilliant relationship with my significant other.

Much obliged Marc and Holy messenger for an extraordinary post!

I generally take something from your messages and this one is the same. Being transparent is a particularly central issue. I've come to learn following 17 years of marriage you need to let each other in, even to those spots you'd much prefer keep stowed away. Permit one another to be powerless. It's in those most unimaginable minutes we can gain from each other and develop. As one who isn't happy sharing feelings I've found when I do I'm letting my walls down to permit the potential chance to see the genuine me. The clairvoyance part is so right on track. Thus, commonly I've conversed with companions about circumstances they are having and when I've inquired as to whether they've expressed this to their accomplice the response is typically no. Your accomplice must be the main individual you share cozy subtleties of your existence with. At the point when you can it communicates far beyond having a discussion it says I esteem your viewpoint, you are essential to me, you encourage me. Wellbeing and security are likewise key elements. We as a whole need to have a good sense of security with the one we love. I could continue perpetually, ha-ha. Much thanks to you for your great articles.

Marc and Holy messenger, I simply needed to say thank you for every one of the posts you continue to email me... I love perusing them as they are a delicate sign of the significant things I at times neglect!!

Your book is awesome all around as well, so motivating and ideal for getting and investing down when effort is short.

Hoping everything turns out great for you both all and keep up the astonishing work,

With appreciation,

Marc and Heavenly messenger,

Yet again both of you rock with the tips you're sharing!

Extremely accommodating!

I might want to add you should have a good sense of reassurance and secure in your relationship. In the event that you don't have a real sense of security than undoubtedly you won't open up. You need to feel your life partner has your wellbeing on a fundamental level. A relationship where your sentiments and suppositions are esteemed come what may. Following 17 years of marriage and being relationally repressed on occasion has demonstrated that on the off chance that your accomplice doesn't have the foggiest idea what your inclination it's outside the realm of possibilities for them to figure out you at a more profound level. It has forever been difficult for me to open up however, when I did it showed a side of me that my companion expected to see. I don't necessarily in every case have it together, I'm defective, I have shortcomings, I'm human. Much thanks to you for such an incredible post as usual.

Your decision in an accomplice is the Biggest, MOST Significant choice in your life. It's not the house, the vehicle or some other thing you can buy.

I'm not the perfect example for an extraordinary spouse. I went through an enormous clinical circumstance that extraordinarily modified who I am and my thought process in 2006. It was not to improve things. I accused God and rebuffed my significant other through rehashed moronic activities. I was even in a mental medical clinic for self-destructive considerations.

Just now, following 9 years of clinical treatment and extraordinary self-work am I coming around to my old self. But I'm still far away from where I need to be.

My significant other has kept it together, through every last bit of it. Yet, when its peaceful, and she looks at me without flinching and says "I actually miss the old David" I have no response.

Try not to be me. I went off my own profound end, and brought a many individuals down with me. Thinking back, I ought to have called out for help boisterously and gladly, on the grounds that even now loved ones let me know the amount they needed to help yet didn't have the foggiest idea what was going on.

Battling during a conflict is the greatest maltreatment in connections, quiet is an exceptionally close second.

Try not to be quiet.

David Rapp, you are an extremely daring man. I might simply want to share with you to require each day in turn. The old self you used to be might in all likelihood never be back how you were, yet the new self you are becoming is valid commitment and love. You and your significant other ought to be pleased. Each day in turn. Fare thee well.

A tip I would share is dependably deal with your accomplice's necessities. Assuming you generally consider their sentiments first and what things will mean for them before you, and your accomplice does likewise for you... both your requirements are being met by each other.

Furthermore, I thoroughly concur with the paying attention to grasp not paying attention to answer... it is a hard one on the grounds that our most memorable response is to need to fix or offer arrangements.

Such extraordinary updates, bless your heart.

Number 2 is the one I've generally battled with, however during our almost 25 years of marriage I've seen that we're consistently at our best when I'm not permitting our folks, kin or companions impact our relationship. I didn't wed any other person, I wedded him.

My better half, our marriage and our adoration for one another are valuable gifts and I know I'm extremely, honored.

Much thanks to you for one more sagacious article and I generally gain some new useful knowledge from your articles as a whole. Despite the fact that I am not seeing someone now, a portion of the data in this article is extremely useful and I was considering the way in which I can develop my associations with others, particularly those near me. Also, when I really do get to meet that unique individual sometime in the not so distant future, I will have this to help along that excursion.

Much obliged to you for all you do!

In the event that every one of you puts the other first, you will undoubtedly have a blissful marriage. Marriage isn't 50/50, in spite of public discernment, and assuming your relationship depends on trustworthiness, all along, it makes putting the other first quite simple. Honesty=no shocks!

Going on 54 years, I'm still crazy about Tom Tough! Love isn't time-bound! I for one think the main thing in life is timeless.

Totally Evident things that you've recorded here. Well introduced. Much obliged to you for reminding us.

Much obliged to you. I'm actually battling with my better half on the greater part of these places. I couldn't say whether I can call this a disappointment or that this marriage of 2 years will simply not work out. We're attempting...

Chuckling. You really want to praise the blissful minutes with giggling, and find satisfaction in what your accomplice tracks down euphoria in.

Very much like kids, you want to alternate in the favored movement, or eatery. Make an effort not to get too up to speed in what you need. I figure we ought to all attempt to invest some energy every day causing our accomplice to feel cheerful and as they're working really hard as a life partner.

What's more, above all, figure out how to fail to remember the conflicts. I figure the best connections could have recalled that they battled a month or so prior, however it's the point at which you can't recollect what the quarrel is over that it says a lot about your relationship. It implies you're not hung up on who was off-base and who was thinking correctly, or about holding feelings of spite to just be stirred later.

Don't hesitate for even a moment to be the one that loves more. This places you in the psychological casing to give all that you can to your accomplice and your relationship. On the off chance that you don't feel like you can be the one that loves more, you may not accompany the perfect individual for you. Try not to be with some that you can't be the best version of yourself with.

This is truly perfect, much obliged. Prior to understanding this, I generally felt that I cherished my accomplice more. What's more, I considered it to be a negative quality. Very nearly a way for me to whine that my accomplice wasn't matching my affection blow for blow. Which is senseless. We're various individuals. He adores me in the most ideal way he knows how. Furthermore, I love him in the most effective way I know how, regardless of whether that implies my direction is somewhat more expressive. Doesn't mean his adoration is any less critical. Furthermore, you're right on target, I Ought to be glad to that I'm with somebody who draws out the best version of myself and genuinely feels a debt of gratitude.

I'm grateful for your works. For just about 2 years, they have come to me in the exact second that I am having a similar test. I read them and am consoled that all that I accept and that I am has lead me to the right outlook. Frequently, following your strength is more earnestly. I gained from this article yet in addition felt extraordinary accomplishment in realizing I'm these things to my accomplice, as he can be to me. In any case, how would I express this without fault. He is our shortcoming since he is apprehensive. He is 90% of what I search for however of late he's lying, perhaps cheating, keeping away from... I'm not a loser but rather those things are not who I'm. Without our interchanges, I'm questioning my choices and attempting to choose the best street to travel. Love isn't all that matters.

It's exceptionally a fact that the couple ought to accept that together they are interesting. They shouldn't permit pariahs to remark on their remarks. This ought to be best the Valentine day's directive for 2015.

This rundown is generally excellent and valid! I have been hitched for north of 23 years, and together for more than 26. One thing I would add is to know the normal "rules"- which might be different for everybody. In our relationship, there are a couple - (1) On the off chance that one of us spends more than $500, we tell the other initial (2) We can say how we feel, yet never utilize "Separation". This gives a protected climate to us to constantly communicate how we feel and what needs to end up working on our relationship.

As expected an extraordinary post, you merit a salute.

Much obliged to you for the great peruses. I will apply these in my relationship, I truly need to make this one work.

Much thanks, God favor you.

These are such smart and supportive focuses. You might have proactively addressed this, yet what has truly helped me by and by is having higher qualities that I attempt to maintain. For instance, marriage itself is a significant worth to me, as is satisfying my life partner. These qualities come from my confidence in God, which I understand that not every person has, however I'm certain we as a whole have higher qualities that we treasure in our souls.

Every one of your focuses are perfect albeit number 17 stands apart for me.

Not long from now it is our 35th wedding commemoration and as we wedded youthful we requested the cleric on the day from our wedding is there any exhortation you would suggest.

The cleric said never rest on a contention. Continuously apologize that very day regardless of whether close to the furthest limit of it you are as yet 100 percent persuaded that you are correct.

As we both have solid free characters that have developed into our coexistences it was a word of wisdom that is as yet working almost 35 years after the fact.

What an extraordinary rundown! I love #19. I think it is critical to recall that this is work and it doesn't occur without being deliberate about it.

Gratitude for composing this!

Magnificent post folks! It's so evident that it is so vital to acknowledge every others distinction and love them for who they are without attempting to change them.

You don't need to adore each and every thing that they do, however to completely cherish them.

A way of thinking instructor of mine made sense of cheerful couples as a Venn chart. Every individual is one circle, they each have their own singular dreams and objectives, and they meet in the center to unite their lives.

Another magnificent article, thank you folks for the rousing read!

Love this rundown... it's difficult to consider anything to add that doesn't currently squeeze into one of these. We are hitched north of 40 years and really can't get sufficient time with each even other! #12 is my #1. We dream together, very day, about what's in store. There are such countless more things we might want to achieve and we get a great deal of satisfaction discussing those fantasies. We sincerely commit to responsibilities like dates each Friday that we plan for during the week and grin with the expectation. We are at present arranging subtleties of a house we intend to fabricate when we resign. Making the future confident and genuine is a day to day discussion for us.

Much appreciated such a huge amount for this wise article. I have tracked down a significant number of exactly the same things in my own relationship. I have really met the young lady of my fantasies, and I desire to never at any point let myself fail to remember that.

To every one of you who shared relationship counsel in light of long periods of individual experience, much obliged. Marc and I are genuinely moved by your insight - such extraordinary something worth mulling over. Much obliged to you. We value you.

Totally right on target with your experiences. I'm guarding some of them for my girl.... luv perusing them over n over once more.

Love is most significant in any relationship and the readiness to be there. What's more, with favors from most importantly ought to be well.

Incredible rundown. A genuine rundown of the components of a blissful and sound marriage.

The main thing that I would agree is that blissful couples truly do discuss these things. By discussing sound propensities and assumptions it assists us with keeping focused

(or refocus on the off chance that we tumble off.)

Much thanks to you for an incredible post. Sharing it on my Facebook page!

Wonderful post!

I generally partake in your posts, now and again not right away however as they direct out where I'm struggling toward everyone around me. I'm seeing someone we have such a lot of developing, particularly me and for me that is something that makes a solid relationship; when accomplices are learning together. Finding out about one another, themselves and learning through shared encounters.

Love is a word that gets tossed around foolishly. My accomplice has helped me how it affects completely open your heart and brain to the excursion of being in a deep rooted responsibility. I have tracked down him to praise who I as of now am and it has cultivated my expert and self-awareness. Consolation and tolerance has just fabricated our bond in the midst of progress and also in the midst of stagnation. He sent me this article to keep on fortifying our organization and to recognize our obligation to have a feeling of profound closeness as the years progressed. Gratitude for sharing these ideas!

Much obliged to you for the article... it helps put everything in context!

I love my significant other definitely... and she disappoints me particularly as well.

We have been hitched for almost 29 years now... and have both survived a great deal.

I experienced extreme epilepsy and was on endless medications for the vast majority of my life. Sadly, I don't recollect especially because of the meds that I was all on.

A long time back, I dialed down the vast majority of my prescriptions and had a gadget embedded that at last controlled my seizures. Be that as it may, presently I can scarcely talk. My better half has been very steady of my timidity and failure to talk.

I've likewise figured out how a basic grin or contact can work on our relationship. Much obliged to you for somewhere around one of your places... number 10.

You folks are spot on. Following 49 years, one of the significant focuses we would add, is to perceive and regard our character distinctions. At times, ridiculously unique sort A's versus type B's might respond to doing life like oil and water. However, our varying qualities make up for shortfalls in our persona, and improve our relationship in numerous unpretentious ways.

We value your day to day bits of knowledge.

www.ingramcontent.com/pod-product-compliance
Lightning Source LLC
LaVergne TN
LVHW050338160826
845677LV00014B/3670

* 9 7 9 8 8 4 7 7 0 6 2 1 6 *